THE HOME BOOK

Also by James Schuyler

POETRY

Salute

May 24th or So

Freely Espousing

The Crystal Lithium

Hymn to Life

The Fireproof Floors of Whitley Court

The Morning of the Poem

FICTION

Alfred and Guinevere

A Nest of Ninnies (with John Ashbery)

What's For Dinner?

THE HOME BOOK
Prose and Poems, 1951–1970

by

James Schuyler

Edited by Trevor Winkfield

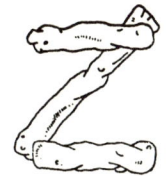

Z PRESS

CALAIS · VERMONT

1977

Some of these works first appeared in *Mother*, *Art and Literature*, *Kulchur*, *The World*, *Chicago*, *Locus Solus*, *The New Yorker*, *Juillard*, *C*, *C Comics*, *Semi-Colon*, *A New Folder*, *New Directions* and *May 24th or So*.

Cover by DARRAGH PARK

Z Press publications are edited by
KENWARD ELMSLIE

COPYRIGHT © 1977 BY JAMES SCHUYLER
LIBRARY OF CONGRESS CATALOG NUMBER 76-52872
ISBN 0-915990-05-9

for John Ashbery

Contents

The Infant Jesus of Prague 1
A Grave 7
Poem 8
At the Beach 9
Self-Pity Is a Kind of Lying, Too 10
The Custard Sellers 11
Mollynocket 13
A Picnic Cantata 16
Grand Duo 26
At Home with Ron Padgett 29
Things to Do 34
Dreams 36
Joint 38
Jelly Jelly 40
The Home Book 41
Today 51
Sonnet 52
Two Meditations 53
Father or Son 54
Stagnation 55
Voyage au tour de mes cartes postales 56
What to Do? A Problem Play 60
Love before Breakfast 64
Four Poems 66

A Head   73
Current Events   75
Looking Forward to See Jane Real Soon   83
Dorabella's Naples Watercolor   84
A Poem   85
Shopping and Waiting   86
For Joe Brainard   89

The Infant Jesus of Prague

I

One afternoon there were hollow far explosions, within thunder, and fire-torn wire trash baskets, messages, understanding.

The shell cracked.

Number: zero to one closed the ring. Duality, eleven, the Roman two. Triads, tridents. Four spun on its unseen center, five, a star, spinning zero, the sun. Etcetera.

Hints, garbled saints, conversion of Jews. Clues in what was laughed at, imprisoned, tolerated, ignored, unnoticed.

* * *

O Jesus let this nigger go!

* * *

Hidden in a lampshade shop, stitching by the light filtered through a silk lampshade-filled display window, the seamstress sewed her plan.

"What do you see?" "A machine." "What kind of a machine?" "A sewing machine." "What do you think of it?" "It is very beautiful."

"What do you see?" "A face." "Whose face?" "My own." "What would you like?" Pinned to a lampshade, the solution to the cryptogram.

"I think we will meet again." "I am very busy." A smile. "You must be." Unspoken word, mother.

* * *

Woven on the hill with orange trees, couples bestow kisses. The sleeves of their shining garments, thick with silver and gold thread, of cut velvet, from their wrists thin as the smooth trunks of the fruited orange trees, of their hands resting on one another's shoulders. A dance in an orchard on meadow grass, wild flowers themselves as faces. No need of sky, when eyes such as these look into eyes such as these, within the sun, a mass of whirling fiery gases.

II

The faster the snow fell the thicker it lay lightly on the town. The sidewalks, the automobiles, the trestle, the best hotel called the Inn, approached by young people in evening clothes. As the shops were closing the dance was beginning. The orchestra was called the Hi-Hats. The young owner of the Inn watched at the door to the bar to see that those too plainly young to drink rum-and-coke did not. His wife, their age, had a narrow chin and a wide mouth. More was suspected than known.

* * *

Bearded and robed, throned in a lunette, he placed on her head a crown, she bending to him, her hands crossed at her breast, like lilies, her emblem.

* * *

"You're undecided now, so what are you going to do?"

* * *

His birthday drew near; or recently past? To their questions, various sets of answers. Christopher would come to his birthday party. Had they not brought him pink roses, one of the two of them said, I have seen Christopher? The day he created him, the voice said, "The one everyone loves, you belong to me." His robe light and finely striped green, his heat blossomed a pink rosebud pinned at his heart. A clear rain of his tears dewed in the petal joints, his sweat smelled of roses, for no more under the flapping of his banner, New Era, would they scuttle, his own family sick with vices creasing their mouths.

* * *

A flat valley, a river flat level with it. Rotting cabbages. The brand name of a chewing tobacco no longer marketed illegible on an unpainted barn. Rain on shale hills, the yellow mud splashing even the windshield of a touring car whose isinglass windows no longer can be snapped to the rusty snaps, if the windows any longer existed. On the edge of the next town the windows of the brick works were broken a long time ago.

* * *

"What is this?" "A thimble."
"What am I doing?" "Sewing."

* * *

He gave his smiles as blessings, platitudinous tracts their readers would look from and laugh, "So that's how it is. It had a meaning all along." Evening, flush from her bath, stepped naked, and shaken buildings trembled alight. Who swam out of the river, trumpeting purple notes? For it was horrible, that they might pray him, mind and soul, into the heart of a doll: bottled, worshipped, that they might run freely in flesh fresh from laundries. Then on, he was seldom seen without a book.

* * *

"I go alone in the city, passing through the crowd that doesn't know..."

III

Dark flakes sank in towers around the street lamps, a rain of May flies. No one walked among the gravestones and stone outhouse mausoleums, but in a bar with a bare wood floor a game of pinochle had been going for some time, and a player was dealt out and another took his place. While the man who was leaving wrapped a muffler his wife had knitted for him and which was very stretched around his neck, three boys in tuxedos ran in without topcoats. They ordered gin and ginger ale. The tallest, a basketball star, spoke to someone who asked why they kids drank nigger drinks?

* * *

A Corridor from the kitchen they sensed boiled milk, the sulphur of stewing apricots. An old man's eyes, pale, rimless as the sun walking into the corridor at seven through the east window. "Mother and sisters died to watch over me. I am like the sun. I don't speak." Hot stewed apricots subside on cold oatmeal into blue milk in a light place from which the sun stepped to go on its route. Later, no letters.

* * *

A singing wreath.

* * *

Across the water lies the shore and its houses, folded like a fan. In the deep coal barge out of the January river wind bearing gulls, a prisoner turns his hands, his palms red through the palms of the cheap black wool gloves the shovel handle wears out so quickly.

Swinging up, the laden bucket spills lumps of coal. At the centre the boards are shoveled clear and gleam gray and silver. Or it is another day on another part of the island, shaped like a stone dividing a stream. Among the concrete grave markers a pale fire, its flames almost invisible in the sunlight. With crowbars, the prisoners try to break the grave markers from the frozen earth. Or they are in the mess hall, eating cake that tastes of soap, or there is nothing for them to do and they shovel a coal pile from where it is to a place next to it. Secretly, quickly, five share a cigarette. Curses flap into the sky like starlings, fall on them like frozen starlings.

* * *

Feast of Christ the King, crowned in Heaven, on earth with thorns.

* * *

Brooding at night in the toilet, he formulated a plan, and let go each new plan as he might a firefly gummed to a spider thread. The vacuum the release left filled with light, a tidal cave. Refracted through water, blues the grotto blue-green of arsenic spray, wavelet slaps echoed to tapped boxes. Any music, than this silence. "Man, you can't love me else I says you can. I says you can't."

IV

At the movies the lovers' fingers entwined. There were no disasters in the newsreel. The sky in the feature movie was blue, changelessly.

An automobile skidded at a corner and drove on. Christmas drew near. Middle-aged men read newspapers on glassed-in porches filled with plants. On the edge of town, on the few streets off the highway that led to a city, newer houses had picture windows, vast panes of glass, and no glassed-in porches. The snow fell like the notes of a harp.

* * *

"Why are you happy?" "The radio spoke to me."

* * *

Shaking out the sheet so it took the air as it had snapping on the line and fell in the watery way cloth designs itself, coarse and white. The blankets to be folded by two lengthwise, like beginning a paper spill; square, like a card-table; oblong, like a fat letter. And the magazines and comic books and books replaced under the mattresses. And the baby's mess cleaned up and the slick terrazzo swabbed with water with disinfectant added to it; and the men waiting to use the communal razors on their three days' growths of beard: many times the cannibal house painter dipped the wide brush and flowed the paint smoothly in long strokes.

* * *

"His mother was a cute sub-deb and his father the richest boy."

* * *

Rain fell like ashes.
"Ver-y ex-pen-sive."
"Please change the station." Or shut it off.
Boredom turned to him, a pack of playing cards in one hand, a book of card games in the other.
But a maple leaf turned white and had one green spot; leaves into hedges like confetti into hair (parades!); far-off neon of towns on hills when a broom pine wound its needled arms around the roundest winter sun; or it snowed.
Violence gathers in a small place: a room, a bed, a glove.

* * *

"I sleep on top of the covers with my head at the foot of the bed. I cannot raise my arm unless you tell me to. Let me stroll, shuffling, always at your side if you will let me. Will earth and sun and moon be joined? Will you take me to your mother?"

* * *

A Grave

While we who wished to help stood helplessly by,
a stranger, whom we neither knew nor loved (saw,
simply, as one of our kind), sank from sight,
drowning, gave up what we value most, our life.

If then between the shifting ocean and sky,
in whose two blacknesses he had seemed the flaw,
had been driven and drawn, tearing night from night
to show us his death's beyond, and ours, a knife!

which did not happen. His agony,
we who stood and watched the threatened promise kept,
could not share, even in fearful sympathy.
Searchlights moved upon the uninjured ocean.
Now he was part of that lighted blackness, slept
in what the screw of our ship set in motion.

Poem

I do not always understand what you say.
Once, when you said, across, you meant along.
What is, is by its nature, on display.

Words' meanings count, aside from what they weigh:
poetry, like music, is not just song.
I do not always understand what you say.

You would hate, when with me, to meet by day
What at night you met and did not think wrong.
What is, is by its nature, on display.

I sense a heaviness in your light play,
a wish to stand out, admired, from the throng.
I do not always understand what you say.

I am as shy as you. Try as we may,
only by practice will our talks prolong.
What is, is by its nature, on display.

We talk together in a common way.
Art, like death, is brief; life and friendship long.
I do not always understand what you say.
What is, is by its nature, on display.

At the Beach

On the Fourth of July at the beach,
the kids from the next cottage
lit sparklers. As fast as they
ran, they seemed from our porch
not to run fast at all. (Spark
stars wavering, the detonating
waves, a hot sky, little wind.)
We sat on the porch in the dark
after the last sparklers, each
speaking in turn till the wind
rose, then went in ourselves.

Self-Pity Is a Kind of Lying, Too

It's
snowing defective
vision days and
X-
mas is coming, like
a plow. And in the
meat the snow. Strange.
It all reminds me
of an old lady I
once saw shivering
naked beside a black
polluted stream. You
felt terrible—but
the train didn't
stop—so. And the
white which is
some other color or
its absence—it
spins on itself
and so do the *Who
at Leeds* I'm playing
to drown the carols
blatting from the
Presbyterian church
steeple which is
the same as fight-
ing fire with oil.
Naked people—old,
cold—one day we'll
just have snow
to wear too.

The Custard Sellers

bits of a Lapland summer dusk

Eve: Night. Night in the mouth of a day that never pulls its tongue, the sun, into its mouth. Tweedy scented conifers, its teeth, curry the backs of reindeers and of boulders in the tundra which is so like a vast body of water near a dye works, sworled with colors, gold in particular. The lichens have a busy summer of it. . . . Getcha custard.

Mr. Bones: Six of one and half a dozen of the other. They call these custards dopes for the caffein that gives them the little kick I need never to sleep a whole summer! When fall comes and the snow falls like maple leaves, red, red-green, and the green albino-spotted ones, I for one will be ready for a good snooze.

Eve: Your money's no good here; these are on me.

Even: (*aside*) At mother's big-hearted chuckle-headed rate we'll never get to Tssk.

Steven: (*aside but not to Even*) Mother's generosity makes me feel guilty for having conned the till.

Eve: All my girlhood in the attics of Tssk I whined for a far place; where could be further? My childrums lead a good introverted rural life, away from bombs and shops and such-like tawdry splendor.

Even: Tawdry-schmawdry. You can't make an ear of corn out of a bag of marbles. Who's for a dip in the tarn?

Mr. Bones: Birds from Copenhagen bring me greetings: "The towers miss you; the dogs with the twirly eyes; the violet sacks of corn meal, cut to trickle. . . ." A fabulous town, sweet little ballets and the sweetest little ballet dancers, Swedes boozing it up on weekends. Ah me.

Mr. Bones: Birds from Copenhagen bring me greetings, strawberries, and straw.

The Mister: The hooves of snakes pounding two-bit pieces into rings like shipwrecked sailors in a prison yard (the sentry strolling, strolling in an olive green kimono with a Fuji fan) opened some puffy flowers at or near my boot in which I had my foot. The lonesomest trail led where roots writhe it out with moles, through the shale and shells of bugs in amber like a palace powder room. Whereupon I shut the book—having written—I forget what—I can't make it out. You'll understand. Tell Dodo Rafferty. (*He falls dead, as though fainting.*)

Eve: So it goes. So after all my two frowzy heads shall see their dream, their Tssk.

Mr. Bones: I'll bury him. I know about these things. Clawed on his headboard, The Daddy of Them All.

Eve: The kids play dead man's float among the slime weeds of the tarn. The sun slides around the sky like a greasy body. Gnats descend like rain on snow. Winter. A tin tram passes, pink and tiny, big with despair; but about what, I couldn't say. It's good to be home, children, isn't it.

Even and *Steven:* Yes'm. We like Tssk, our school and our schoolmates. Remember us to Mr. Bones when you write.

Curtain

Mollynocket

I

Gracia Hooper: Restlessly roaming
Andover, Bethel, Paris Hill
it is told
midwinter night
(raging blizzard)
almost telepathic summons
"Go to Paris Hill"
as if by plan
Mollynocket
sought shelter
in a certain house.

II

Mr. Hamlin: Baby is dying! (*Enter Mollynocket*)
Mrs. Hamlin: We can do no more for him.
Mollynocket: Leave the room. (*They do*)
    Let the stage lights dim and brighten
    As the days will wax and wane
    Let the man child's fever lighten
    As my ointments ease his pain
    (*Enter Mr. and Mrs. Hamlin*)
Mrs. Hamlin: For days you have scarcely slept, Mollynocket.
Mr. Hamlin: Why, Baby is well!
Mollynocket: I must take my leave. I prophecy that fame and fortune will later come (*pointing at Baby*) his way.
Mrs. Hamlin: Fame and fortune? To Hannibal Hamlin? (*But Mollynocket has gone*)
Mr. Hamlin: They say the only good Indian is a dead Indian, But I guess she is the exception that proves the rule.

III

President Lincoln: A penny for your thoughts, Mr. Vice-President Hamlin.

Vice-President Hamlin: I find, in these stricken times, my thoughts turn to Andover, Maine, not far from Paris, Maine, where, as you know, I was born—and to an old Indian woman who once sat dying there. She—her name was Mollynocket—was believed last of the remnants of the Pekquakets who—ravaged by smallpox—migrated to Canada. Preferring to remain in Maine, Mollynocket, when I was a child—a mere babe in arms—once saved my life.

President Lincoln: And thereby hangs a tale, I bet.

Vice-President Hamlin: Yes, and it is a curious one . . .

IV

Doctor: The end is near.

Neighbor Woman: Yes, doctor, though there's little enough signs of change. For days she's scarcely slept. She just sits and looks into the distance, her hands never leaving that deerskin pouch she holds on her lap. Doubtless it has in it herb medicines and ointments such as the Pekquakets were famed for.

Doctor: I will speak gently to her. Mollynocket, the end is near.

Mollynocket: What year is it?

Doctor: 1815.

Neighbor Woman: 1816.

Doctor: I beg your pardon. 1816.

Mollynocket: (*after a thoughtful pause*) I am 100 years old.

Doctor: Have you anything to tell us, Mollynocket?

Mollynocket: Yes.
>
> Where the stinking kittiwake
> And the loud incessant gull
> Hear the seething waters break
> With a "Boom!" so loud, yet dull

> Where the wind-uprooted spruce
> By our banquet shell-heaps lie
> Where the white man tells the truth
> Goes Mollynocket, for I die. (*She dies*)

Doctor: The last, I believe, of her tribe.
Neighbor Woman: A famous princess, and Indian "doctor."
Doctor: Yes, some of those old women knew of things we doctors . . .

Epilogue

Gracia Hooper: And so, in holding its annual summer bazaar this year, Bethel, Maine, salutes that famous "doctor" of the eighteenth century—Mollynocket. As a matter of fact, I was a friend of Mr. Hamlin's son at the Hale and Hamlin law office in Ellsworth. Mr. Hamlin was a fine lawyer.

The End

A Picnic Cantata

I

I feel funny today
but you know what they say:
falls to the floor,
comes to the door.

Who is it you think
might come to the door?
Not the laundry man,
it isn't Monday.
Not the meter reader,
they don't work on Sunday.
Not my cleaning lady,
it isn't Friday.
It might be a mailman
with a special letter,
or a flower shop boy
bringing flowers
from I wonder who?

Or it might be a friend.
It is Sunday.

It is Sunday,
but it's awfully early
for Sunday callers.

Knock, knock.
Who's there?
Open the door.
Open the door who?

Open the door and see.
Good morning, dear,
good morning you,
we thought it might be nice
if you and she
came with me
and we went Sunday driving.

We could make a lunch
and eat a picnic
outside in the sun.

A spring picnic
what a lovely idea
the day is ideal.
What shall we take?
All kinds of things
that are nice to eat.

In the picnic basket I want to find
a roll of lemon rind,
steak and chips,
a T-bone fish,
Milady's Blintzes with white wine sauce
and a pound of Child's creamoginized chocolates.

Four washable plates
and four cloth forks

and lots of napkins.
Napkins are the best part of a picnic.

We can't go on a picnic
without ketchup and a car.
Have you got a car?

You are in my car.

So we are.

Reach me a road map
and I'll map a route.
I love mapping routes
on road maps.
Which route are we on?

Z 3

Let's see.
We ought to be
on 3 B.
Turn left
at 11 F,
stay on that
til you see a hill shaped like a hat.
We can eat our lunch at Hat Hill Park.

My favorite park, named for Henry Hat.
Read what it says about him on the map.

II

In our search for order
the way is dangerous.
To help us he brought us
master masons of Chartres.

He bent to no tyrant,
he never relented.
Among them all and among us
his free spirit may find it good,
more shared, more deeply understood.
Man is no longer the servant
nor the victim of many minds.

He doesn't sound like the sort of person
                          you might find
eating a picnic lunch on a Sunday in a park.

Fried chicken and champagne.

Maple syrup and wheats.

Are you hungry already?

I was hungry at the start.

Well here we are.

Are we here already?

We are at
Hat Hill Park.

In sun and shade
on picnic tables
lunches are laid
where cowboys ride
a teeter-totter.

Hot dogs sizzle
on pointed sticks,
root beer fizzes
in paper cups,
and napkins fly.

Good old country air. You can't beat it.
Out upon the air ride kites
blown, it seems, from rooms in clouds,
their trailing tails of knotted wings of cloth
switching the highest leaves.
Then the draught fails
and the kites fall.

Up into the air rise cries
born, it seems, like milkweed seed
that float on the most lightly stirring air
miles from their field and pod.
Then the wind drops
and sounds are lost.

I read in a big-little nature book
that the best way to make a fire
is out of wood.
You get the wood.

There are five kinds of pie.
Which kind will you prefer?

I will surely die
if I eat any pie,
but I can't resist
a slice of cherry.

How flaky the crust,
how moist the filling.

Now we have eaten
who will amuse us?

I will ask your stars
what is in store.
Your stars today
have much to say.

III

Happy birthday Taurus!
The recent weeks
should have been
good ones for you.

Work hard during
the coming year.
The returns should be
the best in some years.

During the summer
take care in July
and use diplomacy:
there may be plenty
of trouble around.

Happy birthday Gemini!
This can be a big point
in a peak year for you.
You always have so many
things you want to do.

Quick on the uptake,
you don't waste time.
You will have a chance
to indulge in good times.
You need to get in there,
get around and be seen.
In the early fall
you may have to readjust.
But on the whole
the year is yours to push.

IV

The Sunday paper is full of news.
Here is a letter, sad as a blues.

I have a heart problem, writes E Q.

I knew this other man was married
and had a little boy.
He knew I was married
and mother of three.
But we went out together
and discovered
we had many things in common.

Before we realized it
we had to see each other
at least every other day.
We found a kind of love
we'd never known before.
I had to leave him to
come back to my husband.
I felt it only fair to
be honest with my husband.

My husband and I are planning
on moving to this town.
The other man lives there.
I know that we can never
be free to marry
each other
because of the children.
Do you think it
would be a wise move?

v

I never miss the garden section.
It describes heaven to perfection.

Exquisite as a Java sunset,
graceful as a Polynesian dance,
these huge beauties
larger than a dinner plate
burst into bloom
ninety days after planting.

Bali island red
Samoa pink coral
sands of Tahiti white
greenhouse beauty outdoors
larger than a silver dollar.

Stately colorful Darwins
touched with green,
glistening ebony black and maroon,
tulips in balanced color,
flame pink, shaded rose,
glowing orange, shaded yellow,

big plump top-quality bulbs:
all the exotic brilliance
of the colorful tropical birds.

VI

How quick we came
from where we were.
The day is over
before it began.

The food is eaten,
the drinks are drunk,
evening arrives
too late to have lunch.

Rinse the thermos
and burn the trash,
wrap the silver
in waxed paper.

This left-over pie
will keep to eat
for after supper
at least a week.

Oh dear, look here,
we forgot all about
the radishes
and the relish.

The car is packed,
have you got your hat?
Where is the map

and my driving glasses?
I hope the road
won't be too crowded.

Is the evening star
Venus or Mars?
I see it set
in the peel of the moon,
a bit of ice
in an ice-tea sky.

Look at the outline
of the city.
No wonder our lives
have their ups and downs.

How well you drive,
and thank you, dears,
I loved the picnic,
it was loads of fun.
We must do it
again, real soon.

Good-bye, toodle-oo, so long, good-bye.

Grand Duo

An improvisation for Arthur Gold and Robert Fizdale

the Seine
    "transcend, be real"
       she vanished
      "like a light"

                *

Timeless, tireless, sketched, soft
        cleft mountains
        clothed in wolves and conifers
        breathe on clockwork towns
a river enters
petrified sponge
        perilously water falls
        under weeping skies
        rift by a kiss

                *

    Rain lashed the windows of a careening train.
    Tunnels,
boulders, crevasses. Vapors and clouds parted on
    blue.

                *

Art is formality, courtesy, passion, control, practice,
   rehearsing the unrehearsed
        art is no is
           melodiously
           repeated endlessly
           varies naturally

Sweet basic monotone
                heavens of gray
              melt away
green on the blue land   all things awash in jewel and
  beverage colors

                *

Your fingers on keys
sentiments drawn unanxiously
by hyper-accuracy
           Austria! lederhosen, spas and beer
             cookies and the dragon of Klagenfurt
     Music! Schubert! Song!
       a bird declining the verb to be
Florence teaching a child to sing
         nightingale
in German so around sung silence
         nightingales in silence sing

                *

Schubert put his spectacle on
He wrote, *Grand Duo*. Probably,
a four-hand version of a lost symphony. Anyone
may hear it only if you play it.
                  Life
              methodical
            unquenchable
  (meadows dress themselves in green and daisies
    kine fodder. A smiling boy points out the
      way to town)
              in rainbows
       after rain, in rain, letters, a recipe

                *

Summers in town are unnatural.
So is the beach. The sun
flushes the cheek of a peach.
     A gesture in the air
    unhectoring as a smile
      "be quick prolong"
Rapt in a hoked-up coda dream
tumultuous applause of piano history
  the first forte was played on an instrument
built out of wood that marched back from Dunsinane

    Schubert

Franz Schubert

At Home with Ron Padgett

RON PADGETT lives in a quiet section of old Southampton, near the Truth Chapel. The poet greeted me at the door, ushered me into the drawing room with an invitation to sit anywhere. The room was pleasant, but not overly impressive. It is an orange-painted room with several racks of records and sparsely populated bookcases of paperbacks covering subjects from Rabelais to Zen Macrobiotics. The only chair was occupied by a dog. An ivory and gold piano stood in the corner draped with a fringed shawl, two arrangements of white flowers and a nude statue of Mr. Padgett. Sunlight sifted through two windows.

Ron Padgett is a startlingly handsome man with alabaster skin, wide-set sapphire blue eyes, framed with black tortoise shell eyeglasses, and a trace of an accent. He extended a freshly manicured hand and seated himself, smoothing the folds of his pale green Lee Riders.

For a quick moment before he spoke I wondered if I were faced with a stand-in, a man some forty years younger than Mr. Padgett's chronological age. I murmured a favorable comment about the room.

"I have this house down at the beach, but somehow I feel more comfortable here. Down there I have a lot more people around me. In this setting, I can think." His low-pitched cadence seemed more befitting a Southern-bred gentleman than a native.

I wondered aloud if he had heard of the wine inspector who said once, "The 1921 vintages were like Ron Padgett, fully developed from the start."

"I don't drink and I don't smoke, but I think I should have tasted that," he said with a laugh.

I asked him how it felt to be the only poet of the New York School to have his name in the dictionary? He pointed to my pencil and note paper. "You listen and then you take your notes." He said he has an aversion to tape recorders or interviewers who scribble notes incessantly.

Own Interests

Padgett says he writes about what interests him, but not exclusively, of course. He is presently interested in Zen and current writers like Ginsberg, William Burroughs and Richard Brautigan.

"Personally, you could throw out everything from Shakespeare to the twentieth century, except Blake. But some people are into seventeenth, eighteenth century stuff. Let them carry the load," he said with a smile. He said he called his latest book (his first since publishing *Sandwich Factory for a Lunch Wagon* in 1937) *White Light* because "that's what you see when you reach a stage of pure consciousness."

At twenty-seven, Padgett had already become disaffected with taking orders and doing things he didn't particularly want to do. After graduating from the University of Syracuse and getting an M.A. at the University of Iowa, he taught English at Northern Michigan University for twenty-eight years and the University of Wyoming for a decade and a half.

"But I got sick of universities and bureaucracies," he said. "They just grind out people to fit the establishment set-up, and when you're one who thinks that set-up is corrupt anyway, that isn't a very encouraging prospect. The products are just technocrats. In Wyoming the faculty and administration were critical of my life-style, so I left." His experience would not seem to be a total failure, however, because he married one of his students. She now lives with him and is a successful homemaker in her own right.

Works Mill with Wife

He drove cabs in Eugene, Oregon, next. After that he and his wife worked in a textile mill in New Hampshire. I asked Padgett if the different jobs were an attempt to get a broad view of American life and people. "To a certain extent, I guess," he said. "Mostly to eat—definitely before any type of experimentation."

Padgett then turned the conversation to his garden. "That there is the best garden in New York State," he pridefully disclosed. He included that he weeded it regularly by hand among the other chores he does. Many neighbors and friends benefit from his gardening knack, which is mostly derived from what he calls "tricks of the trade." "For example, if you want good cabbage, all you gotta do is pour a little sea water right on the head of the plant," he explained.

How had he managed to stay looking so well, I asked.

"I'm very health minded. My father was once a fighter and had a gym in our house. All I've heard since I could walk was the importance of maintaining good health and training," he said. "Real beauty and health come from within. It shows up in your skin or your face or your writing if you don't keep your system clean." His favorite health tonic is carrot juice which he consumes in quantity.

"Think of all the nutrients you can get from one glass of uncooked carrots," he exclaimed. This recalled to mind his great one-liner, "The only carrot that interests me."

As for American preoccupation with poetry, he said, "What is it, this teaching how to write poetry to five and six-year-olds? Now if they taught them about health in school, that would be something. What could they be teaching them? They know a lot more about poetry than I do," he said. "You know that person who had the Bible reading taken out of the school couldn't have done a worse thing in my opinion," he added sullenly.

Not only does Padgett work every possible day from early morning until afternoon, but walks to and from the harbor when he doesn't ride with friends, a total distance of two miles. "Don't get up as early as I used to though," he added, "sometimes I don't even get up until 'round 6."

Well Read

Padgett is a well-read man who not only knows the writing game, but keeps up with the changing world and its problems also. "I never got my doctorate," he remarked, "but I can read and I keep up with things as best I can." That he can, as he is knowledgeable on such subjects as agriculture and theology, to name a few.

Padgett chuckled and recalled one time when he was listening to Ted Berrigan give a reading in Hampton Bays. Berrigan posed a question during the reading and asked if anyone would like to provide an answer. "Well, I din't say anything then, but after the reading I went up to him and told him all that he had to do was look under the fourth chapter of Thessalonians and he would have found it," he said.

Asked to recite a little from the new collection, he contemplated his stock boots before complying. He stated the title, "l'Envoi," in matter-of-fact tones and then launched forth.

l'Envoi

Please believe me when I say it doesn't matter.
What happens isn't important in any way.

I've been suspecting this for a while
now and I know it's true. I've caught myself
thinking that being assertive was seriously
important to me. It isn't
and it shouldn't be. I won't tell you
explicitly why I know now that worry
about what will happen is ludicrous.
That's personal. Quite vaguely, it's the knowledge
that my time should be utilized
in working toward a more significant goal.
For those who did and still do
think it's important, my apologies.
For those who knew all along,
my apologies too. And believe me
I'm chuckling when I think how
seriously I've been taking this.

Big Red Apples

Asked where he got his energy from he replied that he just never lost ambition. "If you don't sit down you haven't got an excuse to stop," he stated in summation. There are many things he does to keep busy besides writing and gardening.

At ninety-two Ron Padgett neither has nor needs a hearing aid, and is very agile. His memory is quick and accurate, going back as far as the days when he ran a clamboat out of Port Clyde, or even further back when he used to spend his days clamming with his father. Details and amusing instances of such long-past events are always available.

"At the age of six," he recollected, "I started school in the old one-room schoolhouse a mile away. Big boys, who looked to me like giants, occupied one back row of seats, and the older girls, in print dresses and aprons, sat on the other side. It must have been an unusually large school that year, with some coming from other districts. We knew it was forbidden, but between sessions we called on Anger and Lucy in the nearby farmhouse. We must have been a trouble to them, but Lucy was always ready with pins or scissors, and Anger with big red apples. Never, before or since, have I known the name Anger, with 'g' as in gem, but it has to me a somehow pleasing sound. Those farmers had no college degrees, and never heard the words 'Occupational Therapy,' but they did a noble work among the unfortunate."

The entire aspect of the writing game, from payment per line to "pilfering," are readily available, on Padgett's part, for topics of discussion.

"I'm ninety-two, but any time anybody wants to stop and talk a while with me, they're welcome," he concluded.

Things to Do

Balance checkbook.
Rid lawn of onion grass.
"this patented device"
"this herbicide"
"Sir, We find none of these
killers truly satisfactory. Hand weed
for onion grass." Give
old clothes away, "such as you
yourself would willingly wear."
Impasse. Walk three miles
a day beginning tomorrow.
Alphabetize.
Purchase nose-hair shears.
Answer letters.
Elicit others.
Write Maxine.
Move to Maine.
Give up NoCal.
See more movies.
Practice long-distance dialing.
Ditto gymnastics:
The Beast with Two Backs
and, The Fan.
Complain to laundry
any laundry. Ask for borrowed books back.
Return
junk mail to sender
marked, Return to Sender.
Condole. Congratulate.
". . . this sudden shock . . ."
". . . this swift surprise . . ."

Send. Keep. Give. Destroy.
Brush rub polish burn
mend scratch foil evert
emulate surpass. Remember
"to write three-act play"
and lead "a full and active life."

Dreams

you can't remember, giving a day
a taste, like baking soda—
"It always repeats on me"
"I've dreamt that dream before"
—the morning after, or nastily sweet,
slightly, as low-calorie pop,
or bitter as boiled coffee
or simply receding: "Was that a burp?"
or a low-flying jet.
The said to be boring things
dreams, weather, a bus trip
are so fascinating. "In this dream
I was on a railway—a train—
on a gray day but with blue blobs
      ("Do you dream in color?")
        "Well . . . you knew they were blue . . .")
when a kid threw a rock
and glass flew all over
the conductor: "that was no dream
it really happened."
"You mean dreams don't really happen?"
"Don't ask me. Ask Bishop Berkeley."
He never told his dreams
with a few exceptions, like the one
throwing socks at the ceiling
and when they stuck knew they were mine.
Of course it matters sometimes
a lot to whom a dream is told:
"And there I was at the top
of the palm," her eyes glistened
he a little pale, "swaying and swaying

and the lion roared and roared . . ."
Next week, he had a new secretary
an older woman, a little sot
in her ways. Still, aggressor
and aggressed against, in dreams
in which the dead awaken
horrifyingly, or is it a way
of keeping them alive a little longer
and only sometimes? The horror
wears away like weathered paint,
a screen door slams and there
you stand, young and engaging
again. "I can't escape
the feeling that I saw you"
which once was true.
Or there you are, frowning
a little on the landing
with your clothing disarranged.
Only it's you but isn't you
it's oof: dreams are rather boring
to tell about, especially the stirred
up faintly feverish from too many covers
or too little air kind.
Still, you were there,
in a dream awakening
if not laughing, smiling.

Joint

Veal and mushrooms, wine, a too pungent salad
—like eating anaesthetic—
I do not believe in the legends of food,
I believe in the food.
It is not what carrots are like,
it is the carrots.

The wildwood aisle in church has chapels
of mussels and carrots under arches,
of breasty beets with dirt in their hair,
are lit by strings of lemons
and by fat votive candles in stubby glasses,
smoke and shine of leaves and glass.

"I think we rich should get down on our knees
and thank God we have money."

How the seafood smells, and eels,
how they taste (fried) and lie
in their tank like striated muscle.
Burlap bags of rice
that try to stand, not kneel,
sit open-mouthed and spill
splendor in grains between cobbles.
These sacks will go empty, folded like clothes,
to the country and come back in cart-loads
of frisky cabbage
and of tomatoes, red and gold.
Wine runs in gutters,

sour as sweat, sweet as melons
holding seeds like thoughts
or with seeds in their flesh, like sensations.

Lucky who have to eat
and drink, such as stimulating coffee,
slower than water,
that coats the cup if good and strong.

Jelly Jelly

Summer apples, showy and sugary, mealy and touchy
a finger bruise on the thin skin
brown and silently reproachful as your wife's black eye.

But if September apples ripen
and the sun coats the sights with crinkling sheets
of cold while the waves come yapping
something about "wine dark"
evening primroses in clefts of rocks they lap
in a space labeled, "August 27th, 1965
pay on demand," why then it is
September
when pebbles turn, shedding a summer snow
of salt, palely glowing in the first fall beaches.

The wind is pendant-breasted as a naked Swede.
A frosted fox grape shows
where a bird shat as it ate.
Blackberry canes arch and obtrude big nipples.
And the chaste tree blooms.

Back before I made the egg test
I thought the world as flat and very like an elderberry umbel
full of round juicy people winking and waving,
crying "Hi!" and "Meet you in the jelly!"
or "Under the lid of an elderberry pie."

The Home Book

It seemed insensibly to grow lighter as the night shut in, and a distant and solitary farmhouse was revealed, which before lurked in the shadows of the noon. Thoreau, *A Week on the Concord & Merrimack Rivers.*

VESPERS shortly would be over and the young handsome Irish-American seminarians leave the railway-station-like cathedral for the railway station and the train back to their seminary. A winter evening had penetrated the cathedral to store at the intersections and depths of its shadows its rotting ice, which, seeping through the straw with which it was baled, dripped upon the congregation staining their dark clothes. Near a holy water stoup, in line with the altar and the pillar of light that blazed at the heart of the building (bleak and ornate) a plump priest, whose face described certainty and a will to create happiness and to adore God, knelt skillfully on the wet-looking marble floor; beside him, the young man with him knelt as though committed to hesitation. Raising his head a little later, a face in profile caused to pass through the young man's mind that matrix of savors, to half remember a friend.

His friend lay suffocated by night and a terror his lover would have changed to the fearlessness of not being alone had he been, as all day the friend had hoped he would be, on the straw mattress next to him in his windowless room. At a tall shuttered window of a room beyond his in the otherwise empty house scratched the thorns of the sinewy suckers of a bougainvillea that grew up the front of the house. Recollections shook his room like a boat with cravings for revenge and to be saved, the heights and depths of turbid water.

The sun rose and in the afternoon he climbed up into his garden. Rough blocks of houses with bubble roofs were set among rushes and brown vineyards. There were strings of peppers and strings of egg tomatoes. His eyes were extremely blue, like pieces of the sea beyond the town in the glassy light. If it was winter, why had the almond trees begun to bloom? The pouches beneath his eyes resembled their heavy lids: after the night in which fear had slashed his body with its scalpel and placed its lancet on the most tender centers of his being, his eyes were puffy and prehistoric. The almond flowers were a marvelous, unwelcome pink. The tension of his fears and hatred and of his unhappiness and loneliness shaped very carefully his tight, regular handwriting. He was writing a letter. He sensed that beyond the empty horizon a hard blow was gathering force.

February crumpled its heavy snows into a few used handkerchiefs scattered at random on the sodden carpet from which a bird disentangled a thread. Why had life dealt her such a raw deal? In photographs of herself at college with other girls she was the most beautiful because an intensity of laughter threw open the gates of her face like a water lily, with her Veneida-hairnet-hair loosely around it. Perhaps laughter had nothing to do with happiness: she knew she was accused of acts worse than any she had committed. Someone at the other end of the telephone had spread a story of her adultery, most likely, her aunt, the same day she said she stole an apple her brother gave her off the bushel he brought into town to their aunt. Maybe she ought to dig up and burn the photograph of her and her girl friend in their brothers' suits on the railway track! The snow used to be so deep, drifted over the snow fences under the runners. She would like to take the warm plate she was drying and go in and throw it at her second husband because he was going to come in the kitchen and say "You're welcome" in a loud voice because she was not going to thank him for putting a clothespole she didn't need or want in her closet. The bird flew off the lawn with its worm. She knelt and heavily, with womanly beauty, opened the oven. A smell of apples and ham came out.

"Who is he?"

"Someone in the cathedral looked like him."

"I imagine I have met him."

"I think you must have, though you may not."

The coffee the priest was drinking was, in the blue drugstore, the pale silk of stockings. The hesitant young man leaned his head and put his lips to the straws rather than risk a tremor if he picked up the pointed paper cup in its plastic holder. Floral soap began its embalming and the resemblance became more striking between everyone and parts of rubber dolls in a doll factory. A scarred thumbnail put on their table a green piece of paper, scribbled on in pencil.

"When will we . . ."

The sun hit the sea like a cork slipping into a dark green bottle one-quarter full of wine. He was lying on the earth in front of the kitchen chair he had brought into the garden, and the sheets of his letter had become a wild bed of snowbells. Had he fallen or been thrown? A chair leg simply had sunk into the soft earth? He knew if he lay there the sky beyond the coldness of the wind, carrying its herring and red fish across the island, would fix him in the stare of its stars he wished he believed. It was most comfortable, on the unturned earth, where the thoughts would not find him who waited with the boredom of internes around his bed. He went quickly into town, among coughing cats, goats and mules, to pass the one palm tree in a stained jacket and long scarf, grains of earth on his clothes.

She said, "A great many people are mixed up in it. I don't know how to tell you how much I wish it would slow down so we could get together in one car and come to any sort of agreement, just to agree to try to get along would be fine. There is a little girl in a dusty evening who doesn't know she ought to mind the smell of the horse or not to complain of her heat rash, and another little girl throwing a bitten apple bitterly into a lake that was the lake behind my aunt's house; too, women young, middle-aged or almost faceless going as many different ways as cities have streets. It is snowing in a violet drizzle; someone stands smiling in a sealskin coat and felt toque and shoes with one strap that fasten with a pearl button on a Sunday bluff. To whom could I surrender? Get out of the way, I want to look at my ham."

Her husband came into the kitchen. Outside the drugstore blue serge was being spot cleaned of blood with cold water. His lover waited by the palm tree. A man who was drunk was writing him a letter.

Her husband came into the kitchen and said you're welcome in a loud voice. She said she didn't know what he was talking about. He said he thought he had heard her thank him for his putting the new clothespole in her closet, he begged her pardon if she hadn't said anything and he only imagined she had. She put a couple of plates on top of the stove and said if he took any interest in what might please her or in doing something for the home he would have finished patching the place in the bathroom, she wasn't going to invite anybody else as long as it wasn't fixed. It hadn't of course occurred to her it was Sunday and where could he get patching plaster on Sunday? No. It hadn't had it, it wouldn't: she would rather—wouldn't she—nourish her hatred and resentment than ask a civil question and get a civil answer: she was just like her son, he didn't know which had infected which. She said oh shut up. He said he wouldn't shut up in his own home. She picked up one of the warming plates and threw it at him. The plate missed him and shattered on the wall.

Waterlogged and porous trees, imbedded in the soft steel and blue clay of the evening, hung here and there a meaningless leaf. Buildings forced their way upward like shoots. There is a cold humidity in cities in the winter, a stony dampness, that probably causes more suicides than any other sort of weather. It also creates a feeling of indrawn intimacy, as though in the dark a bird nestled in the palm of your hand.

"Dear Father,

"It is true what I told you that when I am with you many of the questions I think of to ask you seem unnecessary to ask, that if I asked them I also could answer them in ways that would satisfy you. Those are, that is, the questions I remember. There are others. There is also another state of mind in which the machinery of your church seems to me hilarious. But that's in its and my favor.

"I know what troubles me. It is so simple: I don't want to give myself away. I don't want to confess, to say I am my history and it is mine, something I made, because as long as I don't I can pretend that I could change and become some other person I won't ever be. I don't want to give myself because to give is to lose and that is like dying; I don't want to lose any human love or pleasure through a deal with that which is invisible and by which I may gain nothing. After three minutes on my knees I get bored and restless, and when I try to pray I end by feeling resentful, that it is the damned who need His mercy, not His saints, and that He could extend it so easily and why doesn't He? Why should He make it so difficult, when He could easily simply smite us on the head with His love? Then He seems the least convincing figment of the too many imaginations which have produced so much spurious art. Then I turn back to my daily life, my friends, my job, the people in the streets and the abstractions newspapers hint at, to intricacies of evil and suffering and to beauty natural, human, of artifact and atmosphere, and I know if I can deduce beauty I can deduce love and I can deduce Him and His strange reasonable demanding and clement family.

"I am always tired. I am always in a state of suspense. To plan to act is to think of an alternative action. I cannot bear to be alone. The small of my back aches in the morning and at night I lie down in a swarm of plans, dreads and repressed witticisms. I am no more distinct from my surroundings, the people I know, the places I go and where I live, than an aspirin is from a glass of water, except what I really am dissolved in is self-pity. And the split between my sensual life and my fantasy of a religious life is like a canyon whose sides join only in its depths, under the rapids of a violent river. I suppose I shall always live like this, and it is not much, since to live seems better than not to live."

He put down what he was writing with. In his exhausted and morbid, though excited, state he went to a window. The two-story stucco temporary federal buildings they built during the first war and kept using were on fire. The summer sky had faded out in its heat and smelled of spit, like a flatiron. Firemen went in and out. Smoke came out the windows. In one window were sunflowers, in another, cosmos, in another, sunfish. Why everybody watching didn't faint to see a crown of clear flames at the base of the flagpole, to see the flag parch and flame into holes like a letter. No, that was seventeen years before. No, it was a very wet night. Down the street, a red automobile was parked under a street lamp. Near the corner his apartment house was nearest to, a Negro had found in a trash basket a number of fluorescent lighting tubes. He took them one at a time and hurled each like a spear down the street where it smashed and detonated, each explosion followed by a roll of the gray ship on the mountainous gray ocean under the gray sky without gulls, though there were some wisps of cloud that went away. There were as many different yellows as a tree of ripening cherries. Would he ever wet his pants again, before he gave up the ghost and the tension that controlled his bladder relaxed? Would it have surprised him that up above him the stitches were coming out, like a zipper tearing apart a hook at a time, that the suture was opening straight up the abdomen and the delicate guts about to sag and tumble like a basket of wet wash bumping and emptying down cellar stairs?

"My Darling,

"I am drunk and alone, which I am usually not though I pretend not to like parties. I was going to write you a reproachful letter. Now I am maudlin, for I sat remembering how much happiness we've shared, how happy knowing and loving you has made me, and how even a little love, however selfish, makes up for the quarrels, jealousy and suffering. I won't ever again think of killing myself because of you—isn't it odd how everyone thinks me the stronger, which from their point of view I am—and my life won't ever mean as much to me as it did when I lived it for you. The best: a few nights, and sitting writing impulsively while birds flew over the river because I was waiting for you to come to me from school. I love you darling. Bless you.

"I enclose an unreasonably large check, a gift I won't ask you to repay. Of course it doesn't cancel your debt to me, and I hope I have enough control not to stop payment on it tomorrow. You know that I believe in keeping my promises, however rash, even though you sometimes made me unhappy insisting on drunken promises you knew

I never should have made. In a sense you wheedled them out of me, for you know my love and my reason don't jog along hand in hand, and to be with you made me want to make promises.

"Bless you, bless you, bless you again. I must go mail this quickly and go to bed. See that the house is kept up properly. Has the cat had her kittens? I will see you in the spring. Good night my darling."

He said, "I looked forward to seeing you. It wasn't your fault. It isn't your fault that it is more or less impossible to take the pain of waiting and drop it out of one's life like a dropped friend. As if one ever could. I know it's merely nervousness, but who would I be without my nervousness? I could only replace it with a fatal belief. It's the difference between knowing that one is oneself wrong, and believing that wrong has been inflicted on one. I speak sincerely with you, who understand my words and none of my meaning, because you feel my meaning more deeply than anyone. Any two people in love imagine they complement one another. I pick old scabs: one Christmas I walked alone over the bridges in the city and thought how there would never be a place for me. Can I prove to myself that that was then and done with, if it isn't? Because I can name my sufferings, are they diminished, or my happinesses greater? My fault: to judge others for my vices, to demand and demand, to hate my enemies and make my friendships love affairs, to want my love to exclude or include all and be the dark steep down which the sun goes. It's late."

They never made up their quarrels anymore; the quarrels passed. In between they were once in a while surprisingly happy together, at any rate, at peace. He knew that in his state of mind only sleep could help him. Sleep! Where was it? What would it be like to awaken cold, wet, wide open to the light? In the dark, in the furry dark pierced by the rattling of the stars like pills, he bent over him and imagined he lay looking up in his eyes wide-eyed though he knew by his breathing that he wasn't. He lay back, drifting at his anchor into sleep like an island.

"Dear Son,

"It seems to me that one day soon, or perhaps not so soon, you will be enabled to decide. I in no way wish to force your decision or to lay claims on your immortal soul. Pray for guidance, practice tranquility, write down any questions or problems you think of.

"When I am in midtown and have a few minutes free, I find the Mary Chapel behind the high altar in the cathedral a quiet place to pray.

"I hope the devotion to the Blessed Virgin Mary is not a stumbling block for you.

"Call me and let us see one another soon; but please do not feel pressed."

"Dear Son,

"How can I get to be other than I am? No matter how much I will to, or you will me to, I won't change. You imagine that you know yourself in a way that I don't know myself, and it's probably true. But of what use is this knowledge to you? Has it done more than make you hesitant and doubtful of the worthiness of your aims, or given you any satisfaction other than a sensual pleasure when you are aware that what you are about to do is a compulsive expression of yourself which you will regret but which nonetheless you are going to go ahead and do?"

Followed by a mad letter.

They would feel better in the morning. In the morning they felt better. In the morning the schedule said:

"In the morning breakfast and visits with 'members of the family,' including celebrations of the return of memory and of the purification of speech. After speech class, rhythmics and natural walking, washing of streets and buildings after which the cities will tremble like umbels; other group activities. Guests are free to write letters or to strike up conversations, to nap or to lie on their beds and read. There will be a surprise for dessert at lunch. Other surprises may occur, though they will be more in the nature of revelations since you will perceive at their inception that their conclusion was what you had all along expected. A collection of tears of laughter will be taken for those fish that prefer to swim in salt water. Between three and four an astonishing innocence will prevail. Perception of exquisite motives at the heart of ugly acts.

Exchange of secrets. Delicious tiredness, sensations of renewal, satisfaction of curiosity. Dinner. Entertainment. Light refreshments. Spells of aloneness. Moonlit walks by creeks, a true appreciation of willows, scouring of kitchen utensils with creek or shore sand. Sleep. Travel. The visible and the fading. Invention. Dreams destroyed, for you will find to dream meaningless, nor will your freedom of choice in any way prevent you."

When it thawed the dug-away hillside released some more gritty pebbles though they never reached the foundations of the houses that hadn't been finished. If a retaining wall had been planned, as it should have been, there was nothing there to indicate it. Often as not the pebbles were damp and the grit became a thin mud slip. Had the pebbles been underwater they would have shown as surprising a variety of bright and mixed hues as pebbles in a surf.

"Of course I would not wish to cheat you of your sorrow or of one act of this new obligation. Though the daily round may express us best, occasions ennoble, and if we are finally each found wanting that can't diminish your splendor. After all, anyone is at any moment almost ready to step out of the delicate light where perceptions cross."

In among the dunes, where the shacks seemed more sheltered though they were not (the best sheltered shacks are built into and just below the crests of the higher dunes along the beach itself), the surf sounded like a freight train passing in the distance of a hot farmland night. Breakers threw pebbles at gulls and sandpipers; and the rippled trail of a snake ends abruptly on the flank of a dune in a small patch of turmoil.

"A sense of my own unworthiness and coming fall. God give me strength to fall easily with open eyes: 'sit back and relax and enjoy the ride': isn't that what it says in taxis? Tell me the truth—is my love just another way of hanging on by my nails? Clawing at the flesh of someone I love. Oh dear. Of course it is and of course it isn't. Excuse the smeared ink; I forgot your letter overnight in the garden, the smears are dew."

One morning it snowed and since it was the Christmas holidays the kids put on their snowsuits and went sledding. The packed snow became icy and radiant. Through the dinner hour a few still sped across the floors of the paperweights getting smaller up the hill where frame houses bloomed. Later, there were more until there were fewer and none.

"Had I known you wouldn't write I would certainly never have sent you the check. No, I would have sent it anyway. How can you?"

What had the church said to the freshman dormitory to cause its clamber leaves to redden and fall, exposing the withered feet of their vine on the cheese-like brick? Something about communion for all on all Sundays, or about The Disciples of Christ, or about compulsory gym, or about a scrap of lined paper ignominiously working its way into the barberry: "Mon Wed Fri 8. Shirts. Family re allowance."

"A very full schedule these days."

The latest work, it develops, was to have planted boulders and flat and interesting-shaped stones in the graded terrace and then to expose a varied collection of African succulents, pinks and dwarf tulips. It is very quiet on some of the streets, most quiet on the ones of gray stucco houses—such big houses—about to shed a bit of pebble stucco onto the mossy ground under their tall oaks.

". . . humility . . . my pride . . ."

She said the clothespole is working out very well, and had heard the votive lights in the cathedral in the city were mysteriously blown out.

Today

Today, hero, scented and candied like a violet, broken to a split bamboo blind, its rub a dub, ground with garbage, old hats, returns to its left breast the plate lifting hand: a lime white heart, heat smelted, whole, Ethan Brand's. A poker stirs the sky above the river, the smokestack, the mild soft drink neon sign beyond the river. Gulls faint. The tourist boat finally spools the ribbon of its passage of the island city. In the street we look up, even the pickpockets forget. It came. We're too pleased to speak of dog walkings, bags to take down, cleanings, though necessity scrubs its face. A pocket mirror serves, and the vices on the little step of each door palm, so tired, their eyes. Rainbows? Who cares! A whistler takes his thin tune past the shut fish green steepled ugly church, and too many windows to count flutter.

Sonnet

August, tasting of ripe grapes and afternoon sleep,
sharpening, like the smell of boxwood, the grass blades
that yellow an uncut hill a heavier green
while the trees lean in folds and the rose of Sharon blooms
and blooms at each twig and branch tip like a toy tree,
setting a sleepy cat on an after-lunch table
among uncleared plates, white-and-black like the coolness
of the oil-cloth in warm shade: withhold from these days
the rain that made the succulence of which you reek
in haze that hides the furthest view and seems like smoke
seeking, before it is time, the ripening leaves
bronze in your pollen-dusty air that films the sky
and, as the light fades, burns blue, that the hot moon may,
bathing its light in water, find its white coolness.

Two Meditations

I

Gladioli slant in the border as though stuck not growing there and around the square white wood beehive the bees drone like the layers of a bulb at the center of which is a viscous shoot. Small green apples hang from the small trees and under the skinny boughs ducks a skinny boy in wool swim trunks steering a lawn mower. Damp blades of chopped off grass and clover leaves stick to his shins. The mower ceases, the bees whirl their routes higher and he drinks from the nozzle of a hose. The gravel spurts under the wheels of a car, which, coming from between the lilac hedges, discloses itself as a laundry truck.

II

Out of the gray bay gray rocks, close spaced and each a little black green north tree forest. This became denser until it was the color of a hole. The trawler anchored and they scrambled ashore in an inlet closed by a little white sand beach like a Negro's very white palm, the guide experienced and dignified last in laced boots with moccasin bottoms. The clarity of the water relicted a dead tree while he boiled great lake trout in a galvanized bucket on a resinous fire. A green flame. Everyone planned to change his "way of life" until he tasted the fish, which was tasteless. Scales on the dull sand like garbage, or rain. It began raining, a drop at a time, big as cod liver oil capsules. The two boys' knees lichened and their shrills faded high and out into the falls of shot grouse curving into a November wet matchstick field. Burrs, unfinished houses.

Father or Son

Detected little things: a peach pit basket watch chain charm, an ivory cross wound with ivory ivy, a natural cross. The Tatoosh Mountains, opaque crater lakes, a knickerbockered boy who drowned smiles for a seeming ever on ice skates on ice-skate-scratched ice, an enlarged scratched snapshot. Taken, taken. Mad charges corrupt to madness their sane nurses. Virginia creeper, Loose Tooth tanned black snake skins, shot crows for crow wings for a black servant's hat, lapped hot milk, slung mud in a Bible reader's crotch: "You oughtn't read the Bible nekkid!" Family opals, selfishness changed hands. Tatoosh Mountains, opaque crater lakes, find me the fish skeleton enclosed in a fish skeleton (fish ate fish) he had.

Stagnation

Down, like glistering Phaeton reaching our town the day the cops initiated no-knock. You are yourself, you are of land of unreaped corn, unpicked prunes, cherries, farm fruit. The wish you wished a kindergarten day ago (stained cut out paper tulips, in paper pots, loving your face) came true sophisticated abed morning, whose Negro friends, fraternizes with Jews, artists. One way to see what you ate is to vomit. Regret, depression, fear, the Moerae girls, harmonize, you cannot not live. The telegram you called back Western Union to cancel: I forgive you; or was it on Easter eggs (green the green crack on vegetable-dyed greenish white)? Drunkard, paper claws up the floor; burn it up. Fierce relaxations. Afraid. Of—poverty? Lovers wait your letters, your kisses, posthumous works wait other lovers. Password: loathing for what was envied for.

Voyage au tour de mes cartes postales

"A man of words and not of deeds
Is like a garden full of weeds"

Travelling widdershins: The Shelf.
No. The postcards on and above the shelf.
A lurking pale-gray Irish castle by a pebbly river.
A cuboid castle, like something torn down at Battery Park.
A perfect castle for the message on the back:
                  Letter will follow.
It came a long long time ago
two weeks at least. Autumn chat
among the glasses: "I wanted to write but . . .
                much of a mad whirl____
                sick____ (tourista____ (other____
                caught up in mural____ (Destruction of Coole)
                sleeping &/or drinking____
                hadn't squat____
                didn't know Erse for____
                other____
                check one & complete
ah, a button card. A long lashed "20's" chap, slick-haired,
blue bow-tied, puffy sleeved, tweezed, lips a thin red gash,
his right thumb hooked in his belt,
left arm up, wrist in and resting on his waist
holding *The Red Book*
eyes winsomely askance asking, "Ain't I cute?"
He wears six mermaid pearls.
Those at the wrists completely hide his cuffs.
Not so the Indian above
enjoining a bison: "Turn not away your head
                O brown and curly!"

They stand before two teepees and in the sky
fly two sides of a nickel.
Look softly! for above the teepees
among curtains and flowers
sits a saintly Spanish child
her eyes uplifted to the lobby of The Brown Palace
six balconies under glass,
green glass over the flags, palms, vitrines and fat furniture
without people. Hard times at the old Brown Palace?
Or "dim, subacqueous delights"?
Working down the next stud
from seven hand-tinted children posed as
wading, swimming, rowing, diving
GREETINGS FROM LINCOLNVILLE CENTER, MAINE.
GREETINGS TO YOU, TOO. How cold they must be
Maine being what it is, how well they feign!
past the ice-cream-pantsed-and-blazered man
who plucks a banjo
for a fluffy flapper pointing with a pointed shoe
'neath the world's most silk-shaded bridge lamp
to
The Death of Chatterton the glory of the Tate.
"At last, the luxury of poverty"
to quote.
The little garret with
  " " window with
a   " plant
with just one bloom
peering unidentifiably at sad blue London.
The poor dead boy
has had his hair in the henna lately
great rings and strings of it
on the thin little pillow propped on a fat bolster.

One hand on the floor, in easy elegance
one hand on his rib cage, "   "   "
his primrose-lined grape-
juice velvet coat
tossed on a chair,
his face is greeny-white, a phial has fallen on the floor.
Beside an open chest, a snow of torn-up poems.
Cold light falls down upon the bed
composing the painting on his left and upper hip
androgynously swelling in gentian kneepants.
A hint of ambiguity, perhaps,
like Duse as L'Aiglon? Or a bathetic minimizing:
"He's sleeping—but *his face is greeny-white!*
What is that snow? that phial? why is he lying
on the bed one shoe on? O
Chatterton, what have you done?
The very blossoms turn away."
Chatterton, that marvelous boy,
whoever it is it isn't you.
The little scene compels, though not a tear.
A swift whisk up the next stud
of religious bits: a face from an annunciation,
a bit of gaudy Gaudi flamed
like Niagara Falls with colored lights
a Rest on the *Flight to Egypt*
(Jesus eats grapes, St. Joseph
hits something with a stick)
on past (next stud: gallery five)
The Wedding Cake House, plain as a pie plate
sheathed in Gothic tracery and spires,
at last to where the heart is happiest,
Cupid and Psyche, gray as a biscuit
kneaded by sooty hands (I ate that biscuit),

gut to gut
her arms and one of his around
thick and hearty, his other arm raised
to hold a garland above her head
and disclose that interesting flank,
a pit no longer, where underarm meets chest.
The nipple of a soup-bowl breast points up
and across hefty dragonfly wings
that rise with a tumescent weight.
Down his back, across his rump, between their thighs
flows an amazing bit of cloth
or is it an effluvia that rises
condensed into a steam like cloth?
Two *putti* at hip level pound each other.
Another strains as he lifts her leg,
her foot free, just, of the ground,
in aid of entry. Entwined like trees,
This photo of a deliberate swift terra-cotta cyclon
on the back is called
                   Cupid and Psyche
                  Clodion (1738–1814)
           The Frick Collection, New York
but on the pedestal can just be read
                     The Embrace
               Claude Michel Clodion
Embrace indeed, Clodion!
Seventy-six years of it (one hopes you had)
seems a fair share. Passionate, virginal postcard
to whom shall I scribble you?

What to Do? A Problem Play

After Feydeau

(*The scene is an apartment house living room.
A lot of doors. Some furniture.*)

Wife: Of course when I found the letters I read them. You wouldn't have hidden them if they weren't interesting.

Henry: You admit yourself that Egbert is a very sweet person. No one could help loving him.

Wife: No, no one could.

Henry: And so I did. After all, it was before we were married.

Wife: Egbert must be a lovely lover?

Henry: Oh, I don't know.

Wife: I do.

Henry: What?

Wife: Well you said no one could help loving him. And Egbert can't help making love. It's like the sun and the sea: it shines, and the water draws up into clouds.

Henry: But I knew Egbert before I married you. You didn't know Egbert before you married me. It's not the same thing.

Wife: It is the same person though. You know I love you. Don't I give you endless pleasure? You do me.

Henry: Likewise.

Wife: But no one can help loving Egbert.

Henry: True.

Wife: And Egbert is staying with us. Oh, Henry, it seems a shame he has to sleep on this lumpy fold-a-bed! And you know what the poets say about the hurrying tick-tock.

Henry: If you mean what I think you mean I think you're trying to shock me. You have shocked me. I am shocked.

Wife: Now Henry, don't get ahead of yourself. I might have been shocked to learn you had an affair with Egbert. Many wives would.

Henry: I am. You weren't. Besides I think you should have been shocked.

Wife: Well, I wasn't. I was delighted. You said yourself no one can help loving Egbert. We both have, we both do. What could be simpler?

Henry: Almost anything.

Wife: Don't be jealous. I promise I won't take the credit for thinking of it first.

Henry: But I like our life the way it is.

Wife: I'm not suggesting we change our life: it's simply an exceptional situation. We both like sleeping with the blinds drawn, but when a full moon rises over the city, it seems a shame to shut it out. After all, when you think of Egbert's . . . But isn't that Egbert now?

(*Enter Egbert*)

Egbert: You're both still up. How nice.

Wife: Your ears must be tingling. We were just saying the nicest things about you. I was pointing out to Henry the beauty—the way they're drawn and their width—of your eyebrows.

Egbert: Gosh.

Henry: I'll fix a nightcap. (*Exit*)

Wife: (*calling after him*) Don't fix me one. I feel so fresh, I'd rather lie awake all night and feel like this than drink one drop to dull it.

(*Egbert and wife embrace and kiss*)

Egbert: You smell so fresh.

Wife: Do you like it? It's something new called *Sawdust*.

Egbert: I like it because it's light and I can smell you through it.

(*Henry returns with two highballs*)

Egbert: I was just kissing your wife.

Henry: That's all right. I don't mind.

Egbert: If I thought you would I wouldn't have. You know how fond I am of you both.

Wife: Yes!
Henry: I'm afraid we do.
Egbert: ?
Wife: Oh Henry, if you won't say it I will. What he means is that we both love you. I mean really love you. After all, no one can help loving you, Egbert.
Egbert: Many have.
Wife: Loved you?
Egbert: Not loved me.
Wife: I'm so relieved. I was afraid the world was our rival.
Egbert: Is that drink for me?
Wife: Is it true that a drink gives a man courage?
Henry and *Egbert:* Yes, it is.
Wife: What strange things men need courage for. We've all loved each other separately, so to speak. The only men I've loved! I must have been born under a lucky star.
Egbert: What is your sign?
Wife: Gemini, the heavenly twins.
Egbert: I think we'd better think about this thing and talk it over.
Henry: As my wife was saying before you came in, it isn't a thing, it's you.
Wife: Henry won't say yes to us but he can't say no. No wonder I love him so much. He is loveable, isn't he, Egbert?
Egbert: Yes.
Henry: Just the same, if you had a child I would like to know who the father was.
Wife: (*producing a bit of knitting from behind a cushion*) It's too late. I already don't know.
Henry: My darling.
Egbert: I'm so frightened for you! And happy.
Wife: I know you men like to sit up all night and talk, but I need my rest. Besides, while I'm away you'll have each other. Isn't that nice?

(*She leaves the room and then calls*) Oh Henry! Oh Egbert! There's a full moon. Its light is all over the floor and it's beginning to climb up onto the bed.
  (*Henry and Egbert look at each other, look away,
   and down their drinks as the curtain falls*)

Love before Breakfast

an interstellar interlude

Moon: Stahs, cygnets. Stahs, cygnets . . .
Lake Lonesome Gal: Why was you blue last night?
Moon: Was I blue? Was I blue! Was I ever blue. Awk.
Canoe: Someone's rocking my dreamboat. I'm like a captain without any crew to screw. Full of tail, up to my navel in a lake.
Moon: How few trees I count, who don't sell a stah nor nary a souvenir cygnet. So cold and so in love. Planets will rise: but when?
Space: Oooooowww.
Lake Lonesome Gal: I was once a beautiful girl. Now I'm a lake. What escapes me is when the change occurred.
Canoe: Grrrr.
Moon: I've blotted out into plenty of old days when inanimate matter felt tired, tired, tired.
Lake Lonesome Gal: They say you've been loved and loved and loved and you're terribly unhappy.
Canoe: Please not to jig jig.
Moon: Get them two in that canoe: he's giving her a good jazz.
Space: The music of the spheres is heard
     On every hill by every bird.
     Now siblings of the sheep
     In the valley sleep.
     Time asked me for a loan.
     You should have heard her moan.
     The moon opened her umbrella.
     She went cruising for a fella.
     The music of the spheres
     Is pretty hard on human ears.
     It spins out the years
     Like an ear deducing tears.

Canoe: Once I breezed, a sapling, in any wind.
Moon: When grass is wet, and crickets whirr, I rise out of the wet trees. They think I'm so bright: but a lamp can't read by its own beam.
Lake Lonesome Gal: Flap flap. Flap flap. Hanging at my bottom, sleepy fish nuzzle a missing man.
Space: Once upon a dream
a shepherd his pants began to cream.
Not the kind of cream that's made
from milk by a milkmaid.
Canoe: I'm sinking and I'm glad. A quick withdrawal and they'll swim ashore. Who cares.
Lake Lonesome Gal: If you become an island in my middle, they'll call you Canoe Island. You'll see. Wait and hear.
Moon: The sky has got no dimensions. Am I or am I not moving?
Space: Feel free to slide
in me my bride.
I have no back.
I cannot crack.
Moon: Another night, another dolor.
Canoe: Glub.
Lake Lonesome Gal: That's it dear, sink down all the way.
Moon: Truly, were there a toothsome tooly twosome in that canoe-ai-o?
Lake Lonesome Gal: I'm turning into a girl.
Space: The moon flies on like a thing
That never learned to sing.
She thinks she will escape.
I have wrapped her in my cape.
My cape is sewn with stars
Like pretty boys who go to bars.
Let her rise, let her set,
I win who never bet.
Moon: Stahs, cygnets. Stahs, cygnets . . . (*fading interminably out*)

Four Poems

for Frank O'Hara

It's 4:30 in Cambridge

and I have a slight headache
on one side only just
enough for a drink.

What a long time since I wrote a poem.

I want to go to Florida
and sit in a shack on the beach
and feel my teeth ache.

"There goes another one," Joan said,
"who can't get it up." But she's
a sweet girl really under the bags
under her eyes. Oh shit (to quote).

Cambridge, I like you very much
to my great surprise. Oh shit (excuse
me, Frank, for stealing your stuff).

Anyway what I really like best
I guess is just driving in a car
the turnpikes are simply grand
and so BORING I have always liked
capital letters and words like
really and very
very very much. I mean I really
adore them. But (I mean BUT

oh hell) will I ever get it up
for him, and what would come of it
oh shit.

It's nice here thinking about all the men
who have one name in common

Between these lines I write your name
in the name of each hair on your chest
(you were so pleased when they came)

And they did come, all curling together
like wisps of clouds over Cambridge
Really it will be so much FUN
when we go to Mexico   Italy   the Canary Islands,
   the Danish baths
and that place in Vienna
and the one
the rich man invited somebody to
where is it in Bali

The plants here are very green
at cocktail time in Cambridge
and I am very sick really of all
the little concrete words such
as names of colors and effectively
used as in Art Reviews

Darling I write your name
between these lines
Very and Really: oh shit
even my spunk has soot on it
like the snow

I adore you! Let's go to Florida.

And John Wieners' poems
well they're really grand

I'll bring you one
printed on rubber

It's quarter of five
and the Fucking Tree has birds in its hair.

Mass. Ave., Cambridge, Mass.

The Wizard Pink Wick Deodorizer is capped
and the vapor teats of a cloud are over
the gold lantern and the blue lantern
of a white steeple in this flat brick city
you might like. And there goes the whistle
for a silver noon. It's odd, having an emotion
so much bigger than yourself, as though
the world were silk I could fold and bring
with me in an Amelia Earhart Weekend Bag.

> "... this dog's life ..."
> *Verlaine*

We must observe the amenities
even if we are going nuts.
So heat the coffee
and it is time
to get the lock changed.
There is rain on the panes
like the notes of a pianoforte
on the phonograph: it is age and pain
I hate, and death. The rain
falls like the sour strains
of the violins into which the notes
of the pianoforte settle grittily.
Can one really plan to live more spontaneously?
So far as I can tell, some dogs
lead better lives than others.

Frank! Frank!

Afternoon of indecision
in a turgid season
when birds come north can't I see it's time I went south?

But suppose my heart tore in two
like tearing up the only copy of a poem
while night whipped by the train?

suppose
suppose

my sky, my green rooftree, my chimney pots
how much I admire how others cultivate their possessions

and you, white primrose who bloom in the cold

I need an image of my mixed emotion
and all I can think of is Cambridge
flowing around the bends of the Charles
while its water speeds under the sculls

it doesn't matter that much
it's only my life so I'll pack
my dirty shirts, shorts and socks

Goodbye Cambridge,
Goodbye Charles

will you wait for me?

out of my heart flies a smile

that slowly revolves on its tip like a gull
over Cambridge, over the Charles

green bank, goodbye

A Head

A dead boy living among men as a man
called an angel
by me, for want of a word,
spaniel-eyed: wet, with bits
of gold deep in the eyeballs
hidden, like a mysterious ingredient
(c'est là, le mystère)
fringed with black and with black,
thick-grown, delicately thumb-smudged eyebrows
and brown cast on the face
so the lips are an earth red
and the rings or pouches under the eyes
are dark, and all the blue
there is hovers in the hollows
under the ridges of the cheekbones
as, in fall haze, earth,
broken into clods, casts shadows on itself:

except what, in the small hours, shows
the razor's path, its wide swaths
along the cheeks and down below
the strong and bluntly heart-shaped chin
where the taut flesh loosens and softens,
heaviest at the corners of the mouth
turning petulantly down from the fold
that lifts the upper lip and points
to the divider of the nostrils.

This so-called angel
who steps back into the shadows of an empty door
and staggers on short flights of stairs
is filled with a kind of death

that feeds on little things:
fullfilled plans that no longer suit the hour,
appetites that sicken and are not slaked
(such as for milk-shakes),
lost or stolen handkerchieves,
invisible contagion
(such as the common cold).

Within this head where thought repeats
itself like a loud clock, lived
the gray and green of parks before spring
and water on a sidewalk between banks of snow,
a skylit room whose windows were paintings
of windows with views of trees
converging in the park all parks imply;
in that head a million butterflies
took flight like paper streamers and bits of paper
a draught lifts at a parade.

Then they went away.
They went away in a dance-step
to the tune of *Poor Butterfly*
played on a wind-up phonograph
of red mahogany stuck with bits
of gold: right stele for him.

When night comes and lights come on
after the colors fade in the sky,
may he minister as he can to whom he may,
himself or other, give what grace
all the little deaths he stands for,
to me, have left him. He is an angel
for his beauty. So what
if it fades and dies?

Current Events

A BEWILDERING SCENE met the eye of pedestrians in front of the bus depot on the southeast corner of Main and Cheektowaga on a recent Saturday morning April the twenty-third. Dominating the orderly throng, gradually assembled from about 7:30 A.M., was the retiring figure of Miss Bellowes, home-room teacher and class-advisor who kept well in the background due to conducting the excursion along democratic lines with elected officers chosen by secret ballot Tuesday last. Notable for their absence were Priscilla Jones, Pauline Hutchy and Joseph Magoratoro, latest victims claimed by German measles.

Welcome back to class Priscilla and Pauline and a quick recovery to Joe. Your absence was sincerely noted and deeply felt by one and all.

While assigned seating was efficiently dispatched by Richmond Crane, Class Treasurer in charge of alphabetical seating, to avoid hard feelings with seat exchange on the return for better views, your historian interviewed Mr. Olson, our capable driver.

Mr. Olson, of Swedish descent on both sides, migrated to this country at the early age of two where he grew up attending Vocational High in this city. After gaining experience around Army trucks during the Great War in which he did not go overseas he subsequently became a driver for Inter-State Bus Lines not missing a day's work since for which higher-ups singled him out for an award. His specialty is driving charter buses including pilgrimages gotten up by civic groups for which he is well acquainted with historic sights all over our land, such as Monticello, historic home of Thomas Jefferson. The scar some may have noted under the visor of Mr. Olson's cap dates from a fall through a greenhouse at the age of three and one-half. Mr. Olson's father was in the greenhouse business at the time. He is since retired.

All present and accounted for except the above mentioned at 7:45 sharp Mr. Olson shut the pneumatic door and set his powerful bus in motion. It was off on another never to be forgotten excursion for the Eighth Grade Classmates of School Thirty-Six. Under the skilled leadership of Gloria Honig all joined in singing the National Anthem, the School Anthem and the Class Song, words by Gloria Honig, music by Percy Grainger.

At the intersection of Main and North Dakota Boulevard the group met with a mishap. To spare the feelings of present company your historian will skip details familiar to all, and merely remark in passing that if you incline to car sickness it is the better part of wisdom to get out at the beginning and not suffer the whole livelong day. As the bus rolled out into open country a vote of sympathy was taken for the hastily departed. The motion was made by Marilyn Skinker, seconded by Joel Price and unanimously passed.

No notable occurrences happened before reaching the State Capitol and the two hour and eighteen minute trip slipped by unheeded in conversations, group singing, games and bird watching by members of the Audubon Club.

First impressions of the capitol city of our state got interrupted when one of our number took a bad spill getting off the bus. No serious injury was sustained beyond having the wind knocked out of him and losing a button off his mackinaw. In a subsequent interview your reporter learned the button was about due to come off anyhow. This unforeseen mishap brought to the attention of all the controversial subject of shoving. Officers of the Class Council report they intend giving the matter their close scrutiny and undivided attention.

Popular opinion among those who never saw the city before was voiced by Marilyn Skinker inadvertently exclaiming, "It's so small!" and the fact a city of such import is one-tenth the size of our home city and a good deal less counting suburbs in the total metropolitan area takes some getting used to. An anonymous bystander reports Miss Bellowes was overheard to aver that appearances are deceiving. It is true that all they have got to do there is govern things and as Washington D.C. is not as big as New York, Chicago or numerous other cities it is probably big enough as it is.

First stop before taking in any sights was milk-break at the Capitol

Luncheonette. General comportment having been discussed well in advance our class president, Morris Milkopper, reports he is happy to state straw fights, napkin raids and sugar snitching for souvenirs kept to a minimum if at all. Some Indian wrestling between the boys did not degenerate into rowdiness.

During a lull before setting out your historian garnered on-the-spot opinions as to what it is like living in a state capitol from Miss Bock, waitress at the Capitol Luncheonette. Miss Bock is in daily contact with legislators of all classes and finds our leaders much the same as other people except for the voice. The voice in general she says is bigger and deeper. She says you cannot make out the words as there is not any shouting but when they are in all the booths talking it sets up a heavy hum. Sometimes the glassware rattles. Miss Bock definitely prefers living where she is to moving someplace else.

Owing to the informal occasion classmates and your historian did not form into files after roll call outside the Capitol Luncheonette. Instead, profiting by Miss Bellowes' previous experience, all moved in a homogeneous mass across State Street, principal shopping street of the city lined with shops, through Courthouse Square and around the corner to Capitol Heights. All paused to marvel at the floral layout. It shows the state flag flanked by the state arms in a design composed entirely of living plants that later on will burst into a riot of bloom.

Then all turned to marvel at the Capitol itself, an imposing edifice built entirely out of native materials mostly red sandstone and composite. The cornerstone of the vast structure was laid in 1902 following the total destruction of the earlier historic capitol in a conflagration. The dome alone is one-third higher than the one on the National Capitol and made out of cast iron. It is topped by an effigy. Plans to coat the dome with solid gold leaf fell through owing to the vast expense. Otherwise it would be the biggest gold dome in the world. As it is it dwarfs all surroundings.

After making the ascent of the fifty-two steps from the top of which new governors make their gubernatorial speeches more marvels met the startled gaze within. Mere words alone cannot summon up the unforgettable spectacle of Thaddeus Boroughman's masterpiece *Peace and Plenty* carved out of a single block of alabaster lit from within revolving slowly on its bronze base depicting scenes from the early history of the estate in the awe-inspiring gloom under the vast dome. After a respectful silence Joel Price, who read up on it in advance, explained what the different figures mean and how as well as being the best you can do in sculpture it was also an engineering feat and triumph of science just getting it in place.

Around the hall in niches plaster casts of ancient statuary such as the Discus Thrower recalled Olympic days and invited comparison with the city our State Capitol is the most like, also built on hills.

As per previous arrangement, Mr. Carl Krause, one of the five official Capitol guides, took over group leadership. Your historian will not attempt listing the sights he pointed out in the multitudinous halls since one and all will never forget them anyhow. The cases of tomahawks and ante-bellum firearms proved of greater interest to the boys while the Anne Chatfield room of relics such as clothing of the wife of the first governor found favor with the girls.

En route to the balcony overlooking the State Senate Chambers which was in session your historian elicited the following comments from Mr. Krause.

All five of the guides got their start in state civil service and do guiding for income supplement to their pensions. Mr. Krause is of the opinion pensions need looking into. He went on to say pensions could be bigger without the average taxpayer feeling it in his pocketbook. Mr. Krause rates the State Capitol as the most imposing structure on the continent previous to Boulder Dam. He holds it superior to any known skyscraper since skyscrapers do not have domes. Mr. Krause and the other four guides are native born in that city of remote German descent as are most of the people there the original settlers being offshoots of Lutheranism. Mr. Krause also holds there is more heavy eating than any other place he ever was. Dumplings are a feature of almost any meal in the typical home and Mr. Krause single-handed eats a pound of farmer cheese for breakfast.

The balcony of the State Senate Chamber commands a fine view of what is going on. At time of arrival not much was. Each senator has his own leather chair and a desk for papers facing the rostrum decked with flags. The subject under discussion was what to do about some hot springs that turned up on a tract a public-spirited farmer left the state for a beaver and duck preserve. This could be made into a park and general recreation area for people to visit and relax in except that might attract hunters, vandals and other thoughtless persons who would scare away the ducks and beavers from land rightfully theirs. On the other hand who is going to pay for watching it and looking out for the beavers' best interests and so on? Right now we are and while the expense is not incalculable these things add up the distinguished balding senator who had the floor pointed out. A side issue is a private enterprise that wants to benefit people by making the most out of the hot springs. It says beavers do not mind people watching them and furthermore what is now a total loss could become a source of revenue lightening the taxpayers' burden without hurting the wilderness any. Then a very old senator got the floor and started telling about the role of the beaver in building up our country from next to nothing. He was an orator of the old school and used his hands a lot. That is out of date but when he stopped for breath you could hear a pin drop. That is an advantage of old-style oratory. You can drown people out and really make them listen.

Sitting in on democracy in action was the high point of the excursion for the civic-minded class. Since the issue wasn't such a burning one not so many senators were in evidence. Some observers noted with surprise how senators talked and got up and walked around while one of their number was speaking. Being a senator is a high-pressure job and the remuneration is not as great as in other lines of endeavor. People should think about this at the polls. Perhaps if senators got a raise they could concentrate more.

This enlightening visit was cut short by the lunch hour. Many already felt yearnings in that direction and began casting suspicious glances at Beverly Elder, official excursion timekeeper. But the ever punctual Beverly gave the signal right on the dot of one when the historic carillons began their daily concert. At her signal hungry excursionists happily adjourned to the Colonial Inn casting a reluctant glance at the Senate Chamber which many may never see again though who knows what the future holds in store?

The Colonial Inn surpassed expectations. Completely restored to its original state in 1933, it includes waitresses in period costume and a fireplace big enough to roast an ox in. Only native foods produced by the state are featured on the regional menu a copy of which was presented to each diner for a souvenir. Foods included chicken, native-grown vegetables, corn bread and cherry cobbler. The latter was accompanied by the thick cream produced by the cows for which the north of our state is justly renowned.

In an off-the-record interview your historian gleaned some interesting sidelights on what running such a far-famed hostlery is like from Mr. Keal, permanent manager in residence at the Colonial Inn. Mr. Keal gained wide experience in the hotel field before taking on the Inn, his most challenging position to date. For instance, at the start uncompromising plans for serving only colonial foods came up against present-day food tastes and dietetics. People eat less nowadays, Mr. Keal cited, and consider gorging bad for health while way back then nobody thought of drinking the indispensable orange juice or even invented grapefruit. So they compromised by featuring state food with supplementaries. Radiators also presented a jarring note but that was solved in a number of ingenious ways. In his experienced opinion the Inn is much more than just a place to eat and sleep. It is living history, he stressed. All who visited it will concur.

Mounted photographs of the excursionists at lunch taken by Mrs. Parker, official Colonial Inn photographer, are available at one dollar, suitable for framing. Interested parties please contact Richmond Crane.

Following the photographing a postprandial tour around nearby streets filled in the time before bus departure. Classmates noted with surprise that first-run movies are a good three weeks behind our own and ascertained they only have two first-run movie houses. More unique was a sight of the governor's mansion well protected by its typical iron fence and gates. As the party filed by an older woman thought to be the first lady of the state got into a chauffeur-driven limousine along with a man rumored to be the governor's son, the distinguished attorney.

Back at the Capitol Luncheonette which sees double duty as bus stop the group rejoined driver Olson and his bus at 2:45 P.M. sharp. Loading was conducted with dispatch and without incident when checking the roll just previous to departure the alarming discovery was made that two of our party were missing! Speculations were rife and energetic plans afoot for a search party when the two in question appeared out of a drugstore down the street. It developed half the couple finds cherry cobbler indigestible and the other gallantly squired her in a sundae. As democracy was the order of the day the incident passed without reprimand although the self-conscious pair did not escape jocular thrusts and some good-natured ribbing.

The return trip was enlivened by a cloudburst.

Tired but happy the excursionists adjourned home a few assembling at Sweet's for discussion and opinion-comparing. The beaver and duck preserve issue received especially hot debate demonstrating the lively interest our generation takes in state, national and civic issues. Although not put to the vote opinion weighed heavily in favor of the wildlife. Level heads felt a marked possibility of compromise since the question of how the animals feel about having a lot of people around is at present unresolved.

Your historian feels he voices the opinion of one and all in pronouncing the State Capitol excursion an unparalleled success. Considering the distance and quantity of people it is without precedent in class history it should have gone off almost 100% smoothly. The committee in charge rates a resounding vote of confidence but I see my time is up and so will not name them individually. On behalf of classmates I will simply say, thanks.

An announcement. Subject of next week's panel discussion following regular Current Events Club business is, could the stock market crash of 1929 have been averted, and if so, how? Open discussion will follow the debate and those wishing to take an informed part had better read up on it, so be prepared.

Looking Forward to See Jane Real Soon

May drew in its breath and smelled June's roses
when Jane put roses on the sill. The sky,
in blue for elms, planted its lightest kiss,
the kind called a butterfly, on bricks fresh
from their kiln as the roses from their bush.
Summer went by in green, then two new leaves
stood on the avocado stem. The sky
darkened the color of Jane's eyes and snow
wrote her name in white. Such wet snow, that stuck
to the underside of curled iron and stone.
Jane, among fresh lilacs in her room, watched
December, in brown with furs, turn on lights
until the city trembled like a tree
in which wind moves. And it was all for her.

Dorabella's Naples Watercolor

Lamped in a postered arch, her settecento name
unpastes secret matrimonies. Gino Caflisch chocolates
nears. Tell where, where.

The sky's orangerie slushes coffee ice. Apostles
excite a loitered noon. Piazza della Borsa shrugs the
niched white statues.

Dorabella, your sisters? What tree in the palace?
I don't know: which tree. Mothers and children expiate
Persephone's stair.

Liquifaction, gasoline. Debasing an oleograph, a
baby burns. No nose portends: *lire* for the dead, mistress.
Operatic espadrilles: blue.

Capri, Ischia, Pompeii. Dorabella breaks a marble
bull's head, purses, buys striped socks. An inkwell hits
the tiles. Splash. Oh.

Dorabella, your sisters? One sings, one botanizes.
I love tweed with silk, pizza, mechanical organs. Ships
undo me. Squeezed by

thieves, whores, rifled, rippled, the tram
takes home a bright penny, my good luck, and drops
black grapes on Naples.

A Poem

Tags of songs, like salvaged buttons
off vanished dresses, a date
Thursday a week at eight, some guilt
for a cab she not only could not afford but:
pretty immoment matter
greets Dorabella's mounting
or are they subtracting moments. "Surely
should be otherwise, should stop, be
thought about, have other quality
than surprise. When was I last surprised?"
Now more a lilac in rain than a crocus
between her office and some gin, Dorabella
herself encounters numerously,
a not so bad looker for a tied and dyed,
a moustached nun of dubious inner life,
a character actress of no talent and less means,
a swami-smitten dowager needling a dull chauffeur,
or a hurrying woman smoothing gloves.

"What would it be like
to change, sharply as a traffic light?"

Dorabella makes a face
at life, and hurries.

Shopping and Waiting

A Dramatic Pause

The scene is a shop. At rise a clerk is waiting on a shopper.
Clerk: Boys' toys or girls' curls?
Shopper: What color curls you got?
Clerk: We carry only our own make curls, bleached goat, flatters any pigmentation.
Shopper: I want to see a toy for a boy.
Clerk: How old of a boy?
Shopper: Why?
Clerk: How should I know what age group toys to show you if I don't know his age group?
Shopper: Who says he's a he?
Clerk: You said for a boy.
Shopper: Maybe it's for a girl who likes boys' toys. Show me some. He likes the same type toys I like.
Clerk: How old are you?
Shopper: A wind-up bird. I want to see a wind-up bird, and a putt-putt and a picture book that makes sounds like the pictures when you turn the pages.
Clerk: Here you are. (*Enter another shopper*) What may I help you with?
2nd Shopper: A pint of sweet milk, a family-size box Snapees and what do you get for your rat cheese?
Clerk: We're not a grocer's.
2nd Shopper: What kind of a store is this?
Clerk: Here's a nice grocer's-type novelty, peanut butter cracker sandwiches made out of soap can't tell 'em from the real thing. Kid your friends! Fun for the bath! Always a laugh! Soap-Snacks.
(*The 1st Shopper is turning the pages of the book. First there is the sound of a baby crying, then of a lion roaring, then of eating.*)

1st Shopper: I don't think this is such a nice book. It could give somebody a serious scare.

Clerk: Now look, suppose I told you this child you're shopping for is this minute at a Saturday matinee in a burning theatre to be known after today as the greatest metropolitan disaster of modern times?

1st Shopper: Go on.

Clerk: Or that the sewer gas has backed out of your kitchen sink drain and knocked your wife flat on the linoleum?

2nd Shopper: I don't think these soap sandwiches taste so good. They could make somebody seriously sick.

Clerk: There'll be snow on the roof tonight.

2nd Shopper: Isn't this shop a funny little shop?

1st Shopper: I came in to get off the street. I might as well have stayed where I was. This place makes me feel I had been in it all my life and hated it.

2nd Shopper: I remember I meant to buy some glasses but I can't remember which kind.

Clerk: Here is a tree you might like to see. It talks, if you get your face in it.

1st Shopper: Let's hear. (*Puts face in and listens, then withdraws*) It said "Bleachers" and screamed.

2nd Shopper: If it screamed I didn't hear it. (*Puts face in tree and withdraws it with a cry*) It bit me.

Clerk: It bites. We could sell you some anti-venom.

2nd Shopper: I wouldn't want to die of a tree bite. How much?

Clerk: What's it worth to you?

2nd Shopper: It hasn't got a price?

Clerk: Yes, it has. The price varies.

2nd Shopper: Could I buy this much worth?

Clerk: Yes you may. Here you are and here is your change.

1st Shopper: How can you get anti-venom out of a stone?

2nd Shopper: Should I swallow such a big stone?

Clerk: Hold it in your hand. No, in the other hand, the same side as the side of your face the tree bit. It draws the poison. How would either of you like a Down Goes McGinty?

1st Shopper: I was brought up on one. I think after all I want this mean book. It seems to have a lesson about life in it. Instructive for the kiddies.

2nd Shopper: If it's for a kiddie why don't you get a paint box and a color book?

1st Shopper: You want this book don't you?

2nd Shopper: Only if you don't.

1st Shopper: I do.

Clerk: What for? Do you think I made it up about the matinee fire? Listen. (*A newsboy is heard passing shouting, "Greatest metropolitan disaster of modern times!"*)

1st Shopper: I got to use your phone!

Clerk: We haven't got a phone. Besides, do you think your wife could get up off the linoleum to answer it? (*The first shopper rushes out of the shop*)

Clerk: May I wrap the book as a gift and would you care to put in a card?

2nd Shopper: Don't bother, I'll just take it. It's for me.

Clerk: At least you'd better let me put it in a bag, it's started snowing.

2nd Shopper: Why, so it is.

For Joe Brainard

January 1   The air is like a Crist-O-Mint.

January 31   Sunny and clear, pale and empty as a photograph, a pause in the winter.

February 10   Snow before daybreak. The postponed predicted blizzard choked off by cold. Now at noon it's windy and bright, not an interesting snowscape, a kind of gusty glare, the sort of day when the way things look is an illustration of how the day feels. In the house there are trails of cold air, changing like smoke. One current is rushing up between the keys of this typewriter, and my fingers are a little stiff.

Still: bright blue, white, and the scatter of leaves clinging to the privet have an almost coppery sparkle. And the shadows aren't at all blue—that of an elm to the south lies as sharp on the thin blown-away snow as though cut out of gray paper with scissors.

February   Wayne drawing: "It's a ghost and he walked and walked and nobody answered."

Easter   Snow and bad temper.

April 24   The horses next door are rolling on the ground like dogs. So it must be spring. An overcast day with the ocean making a dull distant freight train roar—a funny out of the past suggestive noise—prairies at night, or trying and not succeeding to sleep on a shut-up cottage porch somewhere by Lac St Jean ('45? '46?), or "the terrible boxcars rolling east."

From here I can see just one daffodil, standing in its dark spears by the flat stone (really concrete) which is a lid for the cesspool. And a grackle (maybe) flies down out of the buttered sunshine—to you, the forsythia—and lands beside it. Then a whole lot more land on the grass and go marching about—

The depths of the forsythia are brown as pancakes. But the prettiest is the weak bush under the elm and a copper beech. A transparent lemon mist—"transpicuous" light.

May 13   Ron to Wayne: "See this word? L-O-inn D-O-inn . . ."

May   In a bookstore: "I can't decide if I want to know five things really well or a hundred half-assed."

May 18   Wayne: "I can't play with you you bum I've got boo-boo."

May 30   The green morocco binding of the spring, emblazoned with blue stamping.

June 9   In the night cats began to caterwaul. Someone went out of the house and said, "Shh! Shh! Shh!" So the cats stopped, or went elsewhere. I thought I wouldn't get back to sleep but very late it began to rain, lightly, at first like the small rustle that sprinkles out of a sudden new fog. So I put out the light with considerable content and went slowly, and after quite a while, to sleep.

In the early light the privet hedge to the north looks pitted like bronze that has been in the earth a long time.

Last night I finished Arthur Randell's *Fenland Railwayman*, of which it might be possible to say that it contains not one memorable word, and therefore has a pleasant clarity, like a clear glass of water. Of course there is no such book: "During a long dry spell we often ran out of water, so a supply was sent to us from Wisbech in old engine tenders which were put opposite the railway cottages so that the water could be run through canvas pipes into our cisterns. The water was not very clean—it sometimes had a dead bird in it or little, wriggling creatures—but as our cisterns already housed a few worms and snails we took no notice. Each house had a charcoal filter and once the water had passed through this it was as clear as gin." And there is the clarity, a superior one.

June 26   Delicately and thoroughly overcast, cool above and the water with a rosy cast, and the more distant islands a blue with a low hum to it. That small chip is Margaret Fairley's house on Eagle which has "a toothbrush and wash basin outside the door and shells and beach glass inside."

The unmown grass below the house going toward the edge is speckled with hawkweed, shut and partly open, yellow with a blackish edge below, and a few of the orangey-red kind, one bunch of daisies, and single ones here and there, and worked through the greens and gray-browns a mist made out of clover, pinks and cranesbill—all in the "undesireable" bright beautiful mauve-magenta range. The hawkweed goes in patterns like a milky way, and there is the silver of its fluffy seedheads. And at the edge itself flowers and grass and juniper against water down below which is smooth yet seen to move. Looking just there at the edge one's sight seems to grow sharper or more sensitive like adjusting a microscope until one acquires its rhythm and can see more than at first seems at all to be there.

June 27   Differences from yesterday: the overcast sky is streaked with yellow, Isle au Haut is bluer, and though only the most feathery of the grasses sway, the surface of the water is crinkled and running.

July 10   Today, the color of a teaspoon . . .

July 11   On the window hang misshapen drops of rain which the wind mashes and drags.

July 14   After three gray days, fog storms, rain—gracious and other— another gray morning, but with blue rifts. Or riffs. And a hard to look at thin place behind which the sun is pelting down warmth. The air is too thick but it feels so good after days of cold toes in damp sneakers sensation.

The horizon is blue, a deep fixed blue, like that of a star sapphire, and the hilly islands and mountains are jagged: the edge of a torn piece of paper. And for the space of a breath sunlight falls on my fingers and these keys.

A beautiful sentence: "To the student of manorial rolls by far the most interesting franchise is the 'court leet or view of frank-pledge', because it is very common, because it has great importance in the history of society, because its origin is extremely obscure: so obscure that we may be rash in speaking about it; still a little way may be ventured."
—Maitland

July 24   The fog burned off but there are still bits of mist drifting around in the distance like dust kitties.

July 27   Cool and gray, gray and cool, like a steel blotter.
Aline Porter skies: "The kind of hooked rugs I made were all white, with the pattern shown by cutting some of the loops (like pile). They were around for years and then one day I just got rid of them. What a relief!"

July 31   The other day was so hot and clear that one cloud and just one hung over the south woods as though all the moisture in the air had been drawn up and compacted into it, burning, scorched, metallically shaded.

August 4   Gray as the insides of a buckwheat pancake.

August 5   Last evening it rained before supper, followed by wonderful effects of mist and sun. A bolt of mist unrolled in the air above the *Kittiwake* and the other boats in the harbor. Fog came up off the water low, thick, lapping (not licking, but lapped over) the beaches of the bars and islands like densely frosted turf. And seen through the trees, the nearest blowdown to the house seemed filled with boiling gold, a milky turbulence from which unflickeringly streamed an essence of flame pink and orange, a radiance diluted and stabilized. It lay on the lichened trunks of the spruce and warmed away their woods chill.

Went for a long walk with Kenneth yesterday noon and swam at Skokie Beach, lying naked in the cold water that was a little warm on top and looking at the pebbles and snails and tiny shrimp-like creatures. Hot sun, cool air and no clothes: a recipe from the classic cuisine.

August 10   Chilly Saranwrap and aluminum foil days with beads of moisture condensing on them.

August 20   There is something endearing about a young spruce cone, one that is just ripening, like a baby tortoise.

Looking at the sky last night and the moon in the first fresh dark, just a few stars, bright with their cold flares, I had a little crumpled thought, "Oh well, the moon. It's just another place like California." One's imagination drags its feet as we are inexorably hauled into the future.

August 21   It's the time of year when a red flower turns out to be a rose hip, or a leaf.
> The sun is throwing rhinestones at the bay
> and I, a Leopardian glance. How would you
> translate *fango*? Some days not even sunshine
> helps. Or not enough. Why not go see?

August 23   Warm getting on for hot, calm and clear. Only in the furthest distance a faint haze shows that there is more water in the air than yesterday. The unrippled tracks on the bay reflect the light so much more whitely, like a photograph from space—that's land and that's the Amur and its tributaries.

Early this morning the bay was like metal rubbed by hand to a silky finish. And yesterday at the cove ripples in a reflection caused light green lines (like paint strokes—deliberate) to lie on dark green water.

When I type, the coffee mug, the Fresca bottle, the Clintonia borealis, the ashtray and the cigarette smoke do a little dance like Toto in *Oro di Napoli.*

August 26   On the water a few glass chips flicking on and off—and all the green knocked out and stones with the color soaked out of them by heat and shine. And tomorrow we leave.

September 11   "Patty, why do I always look like
a criminal?"
". . . sideways tree . . ."
"The best way to look at a star is
to look a little to one side of it."
And here I am at the typewriter,
banging away about the silence.

September 15   Hot wind, clear but becoming sullen.
Yesterday to Tunbridge Fair—"The 97th Annual Tunbridge World's Fair" small and squalid. Mighty undecorative country people, many of them grotesque in fact, but good-natured. A businesslike little boy patiently making spun maple sugar candy, and beautiful apples exhibited by no. 7—a transparency of an exquisite white, a faint green to it, like a pattypan squash, and an evanescent coral glow. But white. And the elongated strawberry. I bought 18 wooden blocks for 80 cents—
Stopped at South Tunbridge at an antique shop kept by a nice old man: "I'm a gabber." In the loft a First World War army cot looking strong and useful, "Slept on one of those myself down in the pigpen in Dallas, Texas. Slept pretty comfortable too. It was the smell I couldn't stand." He has cataracts and is going to have one taken off at the Veterans' Hospital next week. A beautiful old house, 200 acres, now for sale. In the little garden a big slab of suet (two sorts of woodpecker came while I was there), elegant white cosmos, brown pansies, and dark red ones, two tomato plants roughly but effectively tied up, and pepper

plants with big green peppers among the leaves. And at a corner a cucumber vine growing up a net. "I'm going to ask you to write out the sales slip, figure out the tax and add it up." We each did. Nice to be trusted. At the end of the shed six-foot delphinium gone to seed, blue he said. I asked if I might take some seed. "Sure. Take all you want. I've got a bag here someplace . . ." He owned the second tractor in Tunbridge. "When was that?" "Oh, let's see. That was back just before the Second World War. 1940." Universal Handy Dating Device.

The other day in a store at Cabot: "You want an old-fashioned hayin' het. I hevn't got an old-fashioned hayin' het."

And: "Old Harold says, 'You know what she's buddying you up for don't you?' "

October 10   A light first frost last night and at 7 the grass was crystalized crunch. The sun came up slowly, mist revolved on the pond and the light hit the western slope and lit up the rhapsodic and enflamed trees. "October's bright blue weather," day after day of it—incredible.

October   The blacktop drive is gray with wet and the reddish brown leaves the rain and wind are bringing down are scattered on it. "Starscattered" if we saw the stars the size of pork chops.

October   THE MEN KIDS (on a wall at Jamaica)

    the unending search for middle C

        fields of fuzz
        the futile cotton of the milkweed
(which is a good deal more like silk)

". . . swept the placenta aside, reached in and pulled you out . . ."

November 15   The first day of winter, or, the first wintry day. On a skinny sycamore on Jane Street the leaves it won't let drop shiver under a mollusc sky. Maxicoats come into their own and under them feet dart in and out—but more the size of rats than mice. Close the dark blue curtains ("chance of a snow flurry or two"), hoard the heat, hear a tired rhumba wind up the stairwell with the lank persistence of a kudzu vine, drink Schweppes Bitter Orange and wish you hadn't, feel kind of good, and write to a birthday Twin.

Last night on Seventh Avenue, a car with megaphones: "Pray tomorrow. Pray for our Hippies. Pray that our Hippies will return to us, to our great society. Pray for our great President . . ."

November 20   Artificial peaches of a late November afternoon and a towering dark wall with one small lighted window like an oblong moon.

Late afternoon, early evening, and the sunset roars into place: silently as an electric engine gliding into Union Station, a dark glass cave.

November 29   That's half a moon a quarter ways up the faded morning sky. In the shadows the fallen leaves are pale with frost and those in the light look toasted. Inside the woods, behind the wild white scratches of the bare branches, there is a dark warm green of a single pine, a homely, inviting glow.

December 13   Lizzie and Peggy Grose are downstairs making Christmas decorations, the Beatles are singing "I'd like to be / under the sea . . ." and at just about noon the sun makes the tree trunks stand out through a light haze of branches. Some wind, just above freezing, the yard is puffy and disheveled.

December   "Coming for Xmas—*The Killing of Sister George*—the story of 3 consenting adults"

December 23   "and possibly local slippery conditions" —the weather woman, 1 A.M.

January 1   Snow, enough wind to rattle the shutters, cold, rather bitterly so. A few minutes ago there were bright blue shadows—Prussian blue, I think—and the forsythia, which in dull weather has a rich hibernating glow, looked like a lifeless snarl of hair from someone's comb. But in the time it took to fetch a cup of coffee all the bright blue shadows went and the forsythia is a golden reddish-brown smudge. The white house through the north window isn't white it's pink, but a yellow pink.

Began the new year reading Darwin's Autobiography and letters—so modest, and so delighted with his accomplishments. A little dumb, perhaps ("The sight of a naked savage in his native land is an event which can never be forgotten."), but only in the gloriously innocent way of a man whose concerns are on the largest and most detailed scale. He often sounds so surprised that *he* turned out to be *him*. The autobiographical part has the advantage of having been written for his family—simplicity and only the reticence of intimacy. He seems to have no scores to settle whatever. I can't think of a book with which I would rather have begun the New Year.

*Printed in Meriden, Connecticut, in May 1981
by The Meriden Gravure Company. Designed by Freeman Keith
at The Stinehour Press in Lunenburg, Vermont.
This edition is limited to 1000 copies.*